The
Peaceful
Dreams
Coloring Book

The Peaceful Dreams

Coloring Book

Calming images to soothe your mind

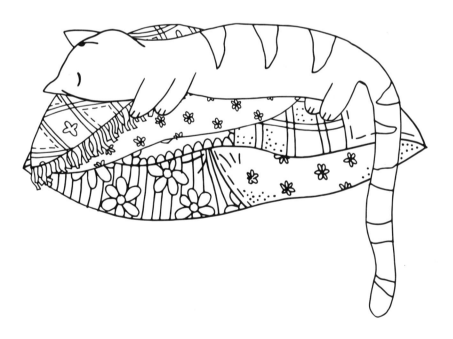

SIRIUS

SIRIUS

This edition published in 2023 by Sirius Publishing, a division of
Arcturus Publishing Limited,
26/27 Bickels Yard, 151–153 Bermondsey Street,
London SE1 3HA

ISBN: 978-1-3988-2840-7
CH011121NT

Printed in China

Introduction

They say that dreams can unlock what you're really thinking. This selection of calming images is designed to help you towards a deeper and less troubled sleep. So you'll find sleepy llamas, snoozing felines, and moon-gazing hares, as well as the odd dreamcatcher in which to capture the results of your night-time imagination. There are jeweled creatures from nature—beautiful beetles and butterflies—and others from fantasy, including unicorns. A multitude of mandalas and patterns with soothing curved lines reminiscent of waves, and others inspired by clouds offer a soothing way to while away the cares of a day and put yourself in a frame of mind to allow a peaceful sleep. Select an image that will help you to feel properly relaxed, choose a color scheme to enhance it and use your coloring time to forget the worries of your day.

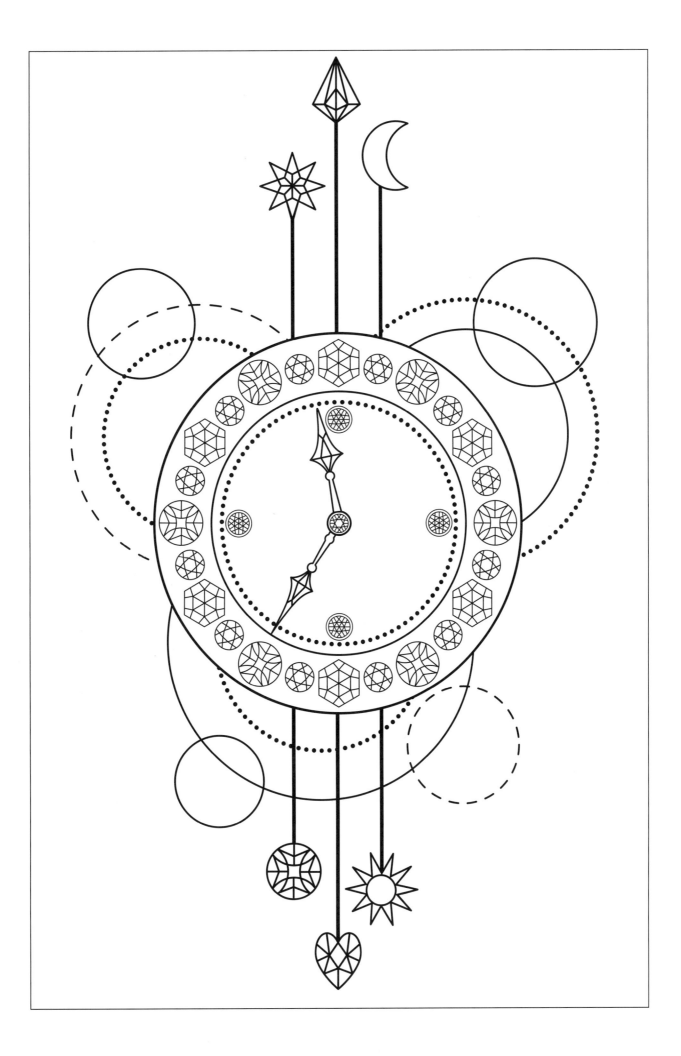

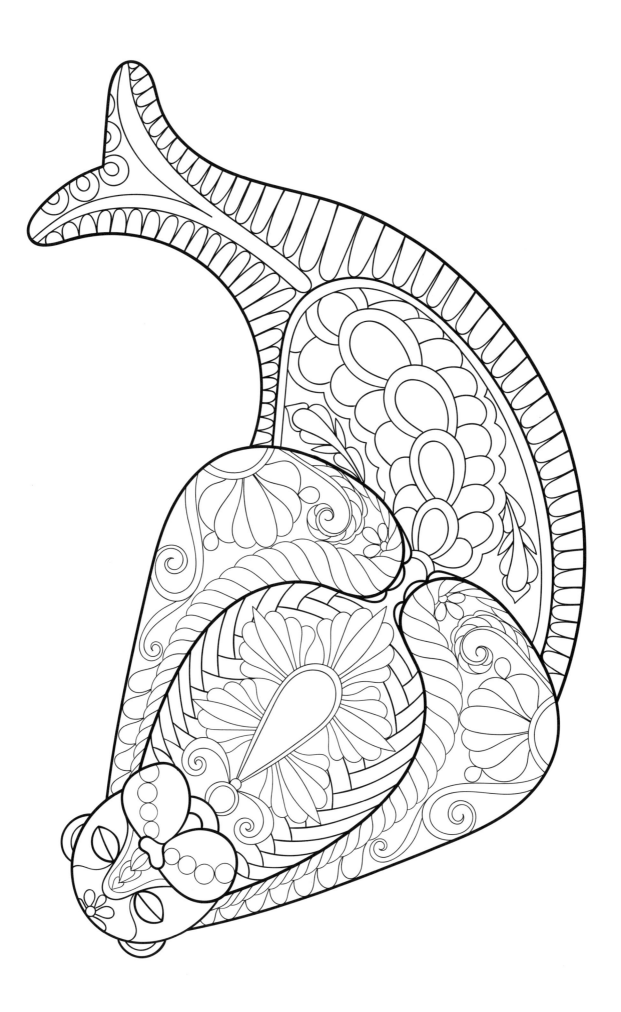

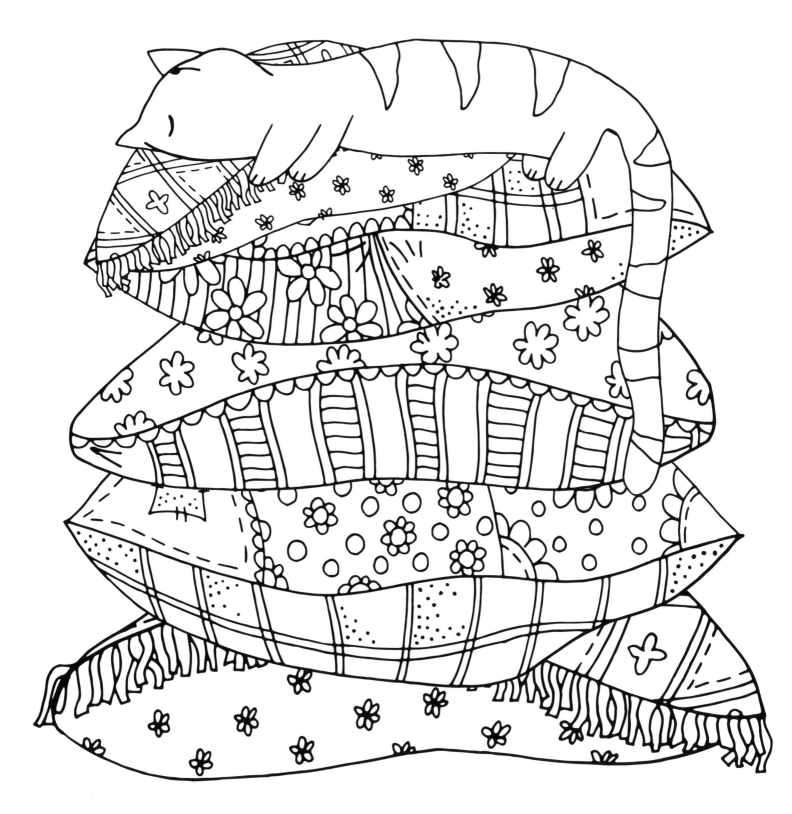

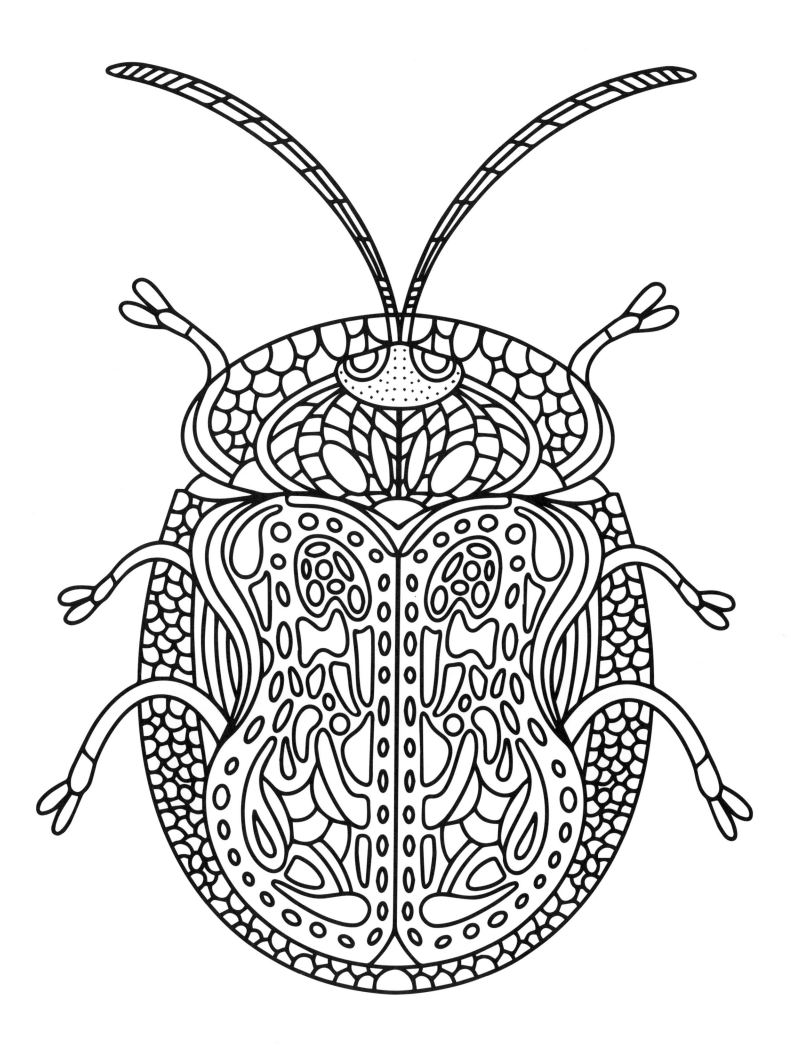

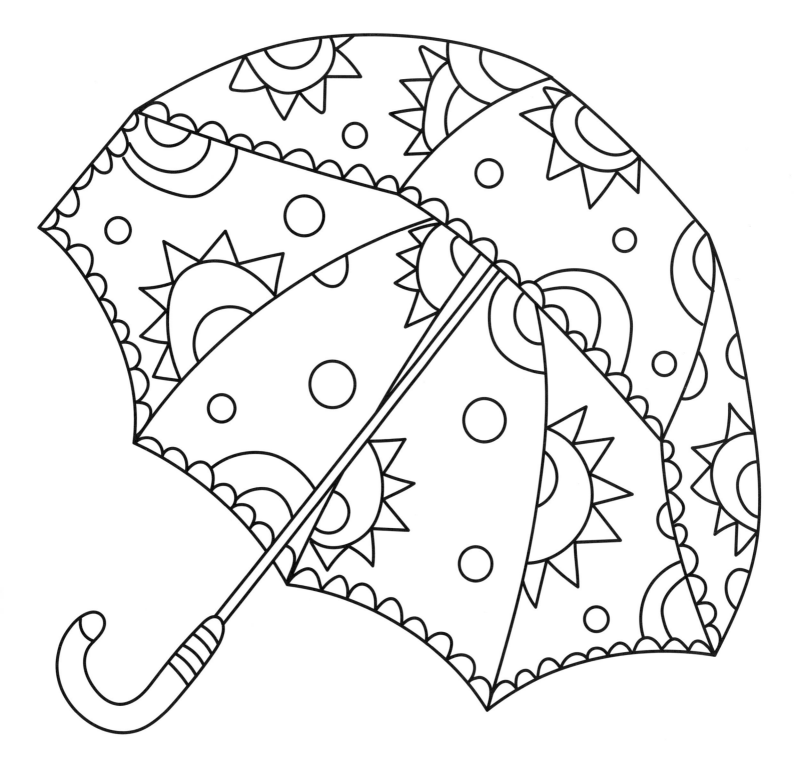

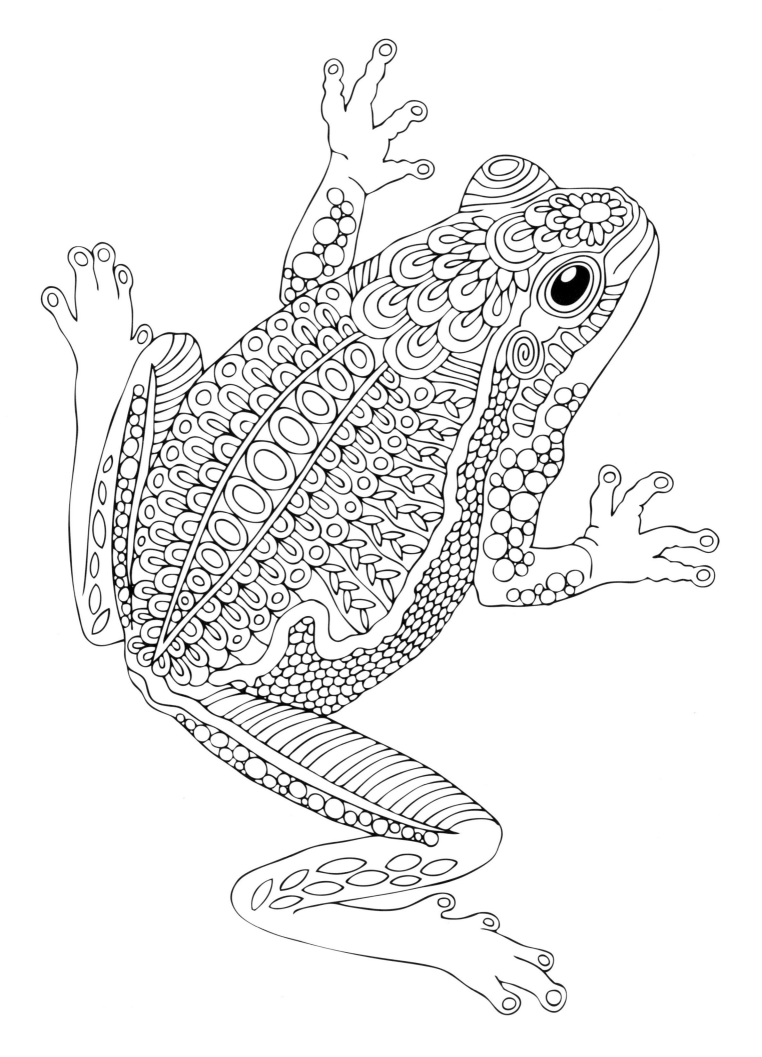